E.P.L.

D0466489

Book Speak!

POEMS ABOUT BOOKS

by Laura Purdie Salas ···· Illustrated by Josée Bisaillon ···

CLARION BOOKS

HOUGHTON MIFFLIN HARCOURT

BOSTON   NEW YORK

Clarion Books

215 Park Avenue South, New York, New York 10003

Text copyright © 2011 by Laura Purdie Salas
Illustrations copyright © 2011 by Josée Bisaillon

All rights reserved.

For information about permission to reproduce selections from this book, write to Permissions,
Houghton Mifflin Harcourt Publishing Company, 215 Park Avenue South, New York, New York 10003.

Clarion Books is an imprint of Houghton Mifflin Harcourt Publishing Company.

www.hmhco.com

The illustrations in this book were done in mixed media.
Book design by Sharismar Rodriguez

Library of Congress Cataloging-in-Publication Data
Salas, Laura Purdie.
Bookspeak! : poems about books / written by Laura Purdie Salas ;
illustrated by Josée Bisaillon.
p. cm.
ISBN 978-0-547-22300-1
1. Books—Juvenile poetry. 2. Children's poetry, American.
I. Bisaillon, Josée, ill. II. Title.
PS3619.A4256B66 2011
811'.6—dc22
201004317

Manufactured in China
SCP 10 9 8 7
4500473670

FOR ANNABELLE, WHO LIVES IN THE LANGUAGE OF BOOKS. —L.P.S.

TO MY THREE MONSTERS! —J.B.

Calling All Readers

I'll tell you a story.
I'll spin you a rhyme.
I'll spill some ideas—
and we'll travel through time.

Put down the controller.
Switch off the TV.
Abandon the mouse and
just hang out with me.

I promise adventure.
Come on, take a look!
On a day like today,
there's no friend like a book.

Skywriting

Line after line of inky black birds

forming the flocks that shift into words.

Page after page of tales winging by,

singing a story against a

white sky.

n the
g-wet-an
ghtly wir

kwor
hat sill
going
it started co
around his waist. "
m so I don't pull her o
s on the string
a

der, the
id the E

me, and later on
you hold
me un again

IF A TREE FALLS

If a tree falls in the forest
with no ear to hear its fall,
does it make a crackling thunder
or descend in silent sprawl?

If a book remains unopened
and no reader turns its page,
does it still embrace a story
or trap words inside a cage?

A Character Pleads for His Life

Open the cover and liberate me!
Turn that first page.
I'll be boundless and free!

Both of us want to be daring and bold.
Make the decision.
Let magic unfold.

I'll help you be something you've never been.
Surfer dude, scientist, sea turtle, twin . . .

If you don't help me, I will not survive.
Only your actions can keep me alive.

I'll swim in the ocean.
I'll breathe the salt air.
I'll feel the waves breaking, get sand in my hair.

Don't close the cover and don't walk away.
Don't leave me squished in here day after day.

Please open the cover and liberate me!
Turn that first page.
We'll be boundless and free.

Top Secret

Describe your desires and they become mine.
I'm a treasure box where feelings can shine.
All thinkers need pages where dreams can take flight.
Reveal all
Your secrets, one entry per night.

ON THE SHELF AND UNDER THE BED

Sharp corners.
Clean pages.
Fresh ink.
Glossy cover.
The perfect book
stands straight
on the shelf
up there.

Down here
    dust bunnies
snuggle with me under the bed.
        Grape jelly blobs stain and
    smudge my pages.

My corners bend,
    slick with greasy fingerprints,
        and my spine is snapped
from being bent
        backwards.

That
poor
perfect
book—

unread,
unshared,
unloved.

Index

Pssst!
Hey, kid—yeah, you.
So you want some facts, huh?

Forget that pretty picture on the front cover—
don't you know they lie?

And the Table of Contents?
That only tells you where each chapter starts!
Pretty vague, you know what I'm saying?
I can give you specifics.

I always say, if you really
want to know what's in a book,
go to the back.

I can tell you the page number
of anything you're looking for.

dogs, dresses for, *62*
magic tricks, *87*
toucans, *31, 86, 122–23*

That's right.
Anything.
I could go on, but you get the picture.

And speaking of pictures, I can
be **bold** and show you those, too.

So I'm telling you, kid:
ignore the rest of the book.

All you really need is me.

Not that I'm bragging or anything.

PAPER SKY

My limbs wrote on the sky with orange leaf pens.

Now I will be *your* sky.

Are you ready?

Cliffhanger

I'm on a cliff—
far down I see
sharp rocks jut out,
waves wait for me.

I feel the edge
beneath my toe.
It's crumbling from
the harsh wind's blow.

Is this the end?

This breath my last?

Please, author, write
a sequel fast!

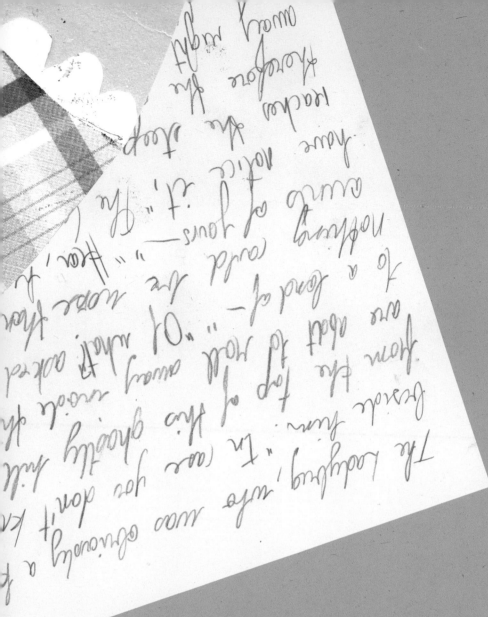

the Sky is falling

What's that big head looming?
Watch—it's coming near!
It's slowly nodding back and forth—
I think it's landing here!

I'm buried under cheek and drool
and hair three inches deep.
My reader drifted close, then far,
then gently fell asleep . . .

on me.

WRITTEN IN SNOW

Snowy pages,
steady track,
tiny footprints
dipped in black.

Through the blizzard
stories roam.
They tiptoe bravely
out, then home.

BOOK PLATE

I don't need your napkin.
I'm not your soup bowl's mate.
I don't want your peas or bread.

I'm not that kind of plate!

Write your name upon me.
I'm a paper love tattoo.
Paste me in your book to show

that I belong to you.

HYDROPHOBIAC

I swallow up dragons and
cannons and
wars.

I don't fear old mansions
with slow, creaking
doors.

I quite like the dark—
murky midnight's no
threat.

The one thing I fear
is the feeling of—

wet!

When puddles attack me or
raindrops are
sprinkled,

they leave me quite soggy—
they turn me all
wrinkled!

I've Got This Covered

I'm the first thing you see when you walk by a book.
My picture is shouting, "Please stop! Take a look!"

I've got dazzling colors—all you could want.
I wish I had glitter and sparkles to flaunt.

I only have seconds to show that you need
to pick up this book, get comfy, and read.

Picture This

I'm the belle of the ball!
I'm the star of the show!
When you open a book
I'm the place your eyes go.

I'm colors and shapes.
I'm an actor on stage,
worth one thousand words
that just sit on the page!

I'm scattered throughout.
I'm the best part to see.
I know when you read
you are hoping for me!

conflicted

I'm trouble.
I'm misery,
problems
unplanned.

I'm an earthquake,
an illness,
a ransom
demand.

My characters
hate me.
They don't think
I'm grand.

But without me
their plots
would be dreary
and bland.

THE MIDDLE'S LAMENT:

A Poem for

Three Voices

THE MIDDLE:

I'm so tired of being stuck
in the middle. How come the
Beginning always gets
to go first?

THE BEGINNING:

Oh, brother.

THE ENDING:

I hate that you're
so unhappy.

It's not fair.
I'm just the Middle.
There's absolutely nothing
special about that.

There's nothing wrong
with being the Middle, really!
It's a nice place to be.

Nice?
I don't want to be nice. I want to be
exciting, *dramatic!*
Maybe I should go first in the next
book I'm in.

Look, it doesn't work
that way. Get it through
your thick page.

No need to be rude.
He's just feeling insecure.

I want to be
the very **FIRST** page for once.
Even kids who don't like the book
will read me before they give up.

That *is* true.
Everybody reads me!
But face it: you're not first in line.
It's not gonna happen.
Give it up!

Don't be selfish.
Maybe you could let him
go first just once . . .

What?
That wouldn't make sense!
The story would start
in the middle!

Still—

Or . . .
I wouldn't mind being last.
The last page of the last chapter.
I'd get to have the **LAST WORD!**

This Is the Book

She is the writer
with dreams in her head
who writes them down
so they can be read.

He is the editor
who helps to choose
which of the wonderful
words to use.

She is the designer
who plans on the look
the words will have
throughout the book.

He is the illustrator
who creates the art
that make the words
bloom in your heart.

She is the publisher
who pays all the fees
to print the book
and hopes it will please.

He is the buyer
who orders the tale
to put on display
for loan or for sale.

And she is the reader
who browses the shelf
and looks for new worlds
but finds herself.

LIGHTS OUT AT THE BOOKSTORE

During the day,
we wait in straight rows.
We're frozen, we're still until night . . .
until closing.

Then the party starts!

We eat treats in COOKBOOKS
and bop to the beat of MUSIC.
We run relays down miles
of aisles of SPORTS.
  Parenting books holler,
    "Careful with that red punch!" and
    "Use your inside voices."
    CHILDREN'S books laugh and scream
    and climb on counters.
  We circle the booklights, and
into the night, MYSTERIES
  murmur fears in our ears.
  Then we gobble up gumdrops,
  tell RIDDLES & JOKES,
  and bend our spines to limbo.
  We party on until dawn.
  We're wired, too tired
  to hoist ourselves
  back to the shelves.

At opening time,
  the owner unlocks the door;
  we're sprawled on the floor in deep-sleeping piles.
  "Who made this mess?"
  But he suspects:
  "Bye, books—
  I'll come back for the party tonight!"

Vacation Time!

Whenever I'm checked out, it's like a vacation.
I'm scanned and I'm packed for a new destination!

I've floated in airplanes. I've lain on the beach.
I've hidden in bunk beds—just out of your reach.

Been stained by spaghetti, been splashed at the lake.
I've shared your adventures. I've kept you awake.

At night in your sleeping bag—too dark to see—
you whipped out a flashlight to keep reading me.

I never quite know where my reader is bound,
and hundreds of times I've been lost and then found.

It's good to get home, look around, see what's new,
but before long I'm antsy . . .

A trip's overdue!

The End

You race
toward me,
checking page numbers
and calculating their distance.

You
sprint skip skim
to win
the reader's race
to cross me—

the book's finish line.

But then
you
smile, cry, sigh,

flip to chapter one
and start again.

I am not so much
The End
as I am an
invitation back
to the beginning.